‹BURUNDI›

PLACES AND PEOPLES OF THE WORLD
BURUNDI

Marian F. Wolbers

CHELSEA HOUSE PUBLISHERS
New York • Philadelphia

COVER: As they have for centuries, Burundians gather in the marketplace to trade news and conduct business.

Chelsea House Publishers
Editor-in-Chief: Nancy Toff
Executive Editor: Remmel T. Nunn
Managing Editor: Karyn Gullen Browne
Copy Chief: Juliann Barbato
Picture Editor: Adrian G. Allen
Art Director: Maria Epes
Manufacturing Manager: Gerald Levine

Places and Peoples of the World
Editorial Director: Rebecca Stefoff

Staff for BURUNDI
Text Editor: Rebecca Stefoff
Copy Editor: Phil Koslow
Deputy Copy Chief: Nicole Bowen
Editorial Assistant: Marie Claire Cebrián
Picture Researcher: Susan Biederman
Assistant Art Director: Loraine Machlin
Designer: Marie-Hélène Fredericks
Production Coordinator: Joseph Romano

3 5 7 9 8 6 4 2

Library of Congress Cataloging-in-Publication Data

Wolbers, Marian
Burundi.

(Places and peoples of the world)
Includes index.
(Surveys the history, topography, people, and
culture of Burundi, with emphasis on its current economy,
industry, and place in the political world.
1. Burundi—History. 2. Burundi—Ethnology—
Burundi. 3. Burundi—Civilization. 4. Burundi.
I. Title. II. Series.
DT450.54.W65   1988   967'.572   87-18272
ISBN 1-55546-785-7

14.95

◄CONTENTS►

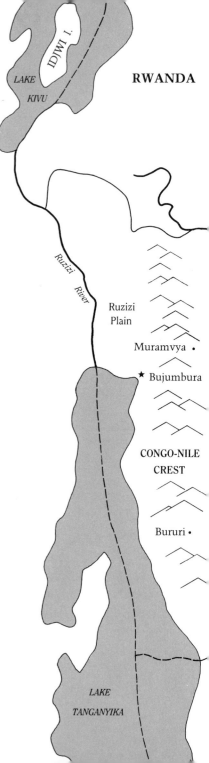

RWANDA

ZAIRE

Ruzizi Plain

Muramvya •

★ Bujumbura

CONGO-NILE CREST

Bururi •

LAKE TANGANYIKA

IDJWI I.

LAKE KIVU

Ruzizi River

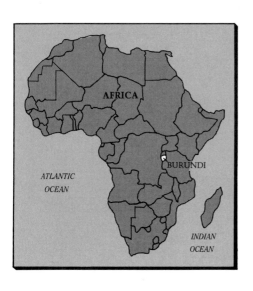

AFRICA

ATLANTIC OCEAN

BURUNDI

INDIAN OCEAN

N

LAKE RWERU

LAKE COHOHA

Kagera River

Akanyaru River

Rugari •

• Ngozi

• Karuzi

BURUNDI

Ruvuvu River

• Gitega

• Ruyigi

TANZANIA

• Rutana

Malagarasi River

Malagarasi River

◄ FACTS AT A GLANCE ►

Land and People

Area	10,759 square miles (28,188 square kilometers)
Length from North to South	163 miles (263 kilometers)
Width from West to East	121 miles (194 kilometers)
Highest Point	9,055 feet (2,760 meters)
Major Rivers	Ruzizi, Akanyaru, Kagera, Ruvuvu, Malagarasi
Major Lakes	Tanganyika, Rweru, Cohoha
Population	4,989,000
Population Density	464 people per square mile (177 per square kilometer)
Population Distribution	Rural, 92 percent; urban, 8 percent
Capital	Bujumbura (population 272,600)
Other Cities	Gitega (population 95,300), Ngozi (population 20,000)
Official Languages	Kirundi, French
Other Languages	Swahili
Ethnic Groups	Hutu, 83 percent; Tutsi, 13 percent; European, Arab, or Asian, 3 percent; Twa, 1 percent
Religions	Roman Catholic, 78 percent; Protestant, 7 percent; Muslim, 1 percent; about 40 percent of Burundians, including many Christians, also have traditional African animist beliefs

Economy

Land use	Farming, 51 percent; meadows and pastures, 35.5 percent; forest, 2.5 percent; other, 11 percent
Major Food Crops	Cassava, sweet potatoes, beans, bananas, corn, sorghum
Major Cash Crops	Coffee, cotton, tea, palm oil, tobacco
Resources	Nickel, phosphate, vanadium, peat, tin, bastnaesite
Major Trade Partners	Belgium, Luxembourg, France, West Germany, Iran, United States, Italy, Japan
Economic Production	Agriculture, 63.1 percent; manufacturing, 10.2 percent; trade, 7.1 percent; public administration and defense, 10.0 percent; services, 1.3 percent; construction, 5.3 percent; transportation and communication, 2.5 percent; mining, 0.5 percent
Currency	Burundi franc (FBu), divided into 100 centimes; 1 FBu equals about 80 percent of U.S. $0.01; 126.19 FBu equal U.S. $1

Government

Form of Government	Constitutional republic; constitution was suspended by a military coup in 1987
Head of Government	President
Legislative Body	National Assembly, suspended in 1987; governing bodies since 1987: Military Committee for National Salvation, Council of Ministers
Political Party	National Progress and Unity party (UPRONA)

◄HISTORY AT A GLANCE►

before 7th century A.D.	Burundi is inhabited by small tribal groups of the Twa, Pygmy-like hunters who live in the forests.
7th through 10th centuries	Groups of Hutu, a Bantu people from the Congo River basin, migrate into the region. They dominate the Twa and introduce a culture of farms and villages.
by 14th century	The Hutu have established many small agricultural kingdoms.
15th and 16th centuries	The Tutsi, a tall, warlike people from the north, migrate into Burundi and the neighboring country of Rwanda. They dominate the Hutu, set up the country of Rwanda, and set up a complex society based on cattle herding. The Hutu are workers, and the Tutsi are rulers and nobles.
mid-16th century	The first Tutsi king, Ntare I Rushatsi, comes to power over the entire region.
1858	Explorers John Hanning Speke and Richard Burton, searching for the source of the Nile River, reach Lake Tanganyika.
1871	David Livingstone and Henry Morton Stanley explore western Burundi.
1884–85	The Berlin Conference grants Germany the right to extend its control of East Africa into Rwanda and Burundi.

early 1890s   Two German explorers, Oskar Baumann and Count von Götzen, map much of Rwanda and Burundi and claim the region for Germany.

1898   The first Roman Catholic missionaries arrive in Burundi.

1916   During World War I, Belgian troops occupy German East Africa.

1923   The League of Nations gives control of Rwanda and Burundi, then known as Ruanda-Urundi, to Belgium.

1946   Ruanda-Urundi becomes a United Nations trust territory under Belgian administration.

1950s   Conflict increases between the Tutsi and the Hutu. The Hutu are more numerous, but the Tutsi control most of the wealth and power.

1959   Thousands of Tutsi flee from Rwanda, which is dominated by the Hutu, into Burundi. Their presence increases the conflict between the two peoples in Burundi.

1961   The first elections are held, under United Nations supervision. Prince Louis Rwagasore is elected prime minister, but he is assassinated weeks later.

1962   The United Nations General Assembly votes full independence for two new nations, Burundi and Rwanda. Rwanda is a republic; the Hutu dominate its government. Burundi is a kingdom, with a hereditary king and an elected prime minister. The king, prime minister, and other leaders are Tutsi.

1966   The king is dethroned by Michel Micombero, his prime minister, who takes over the government and abolishes the kingship.

1970s	Several coups are attempted against the Micombero government, which cracks down on the Hutu population in a series of brutal massacres. Many Hutu flee the country.
1974	The National Progress and Unity party (UPRONA) is made the only party permitted by law in the country.
1976	The army seizes the government, removes Micombero from power, and names Jean-Baptiste Bagaza president.
1984	Running as the only candidate, Bagaza is elected president of UPRONA and then of Burundi.
1987	A coup led by the army throws Bagaza out of office and makes Pierre Buyoya the new president. He suspends the constitution, dismisses the National Assembly, and sets up the Military Committee for National Salvation and the Council of Ministers to govern the country.
late 1980s	Buyoya continues in power. The Tutsi minority remains in control of the government and resources. Violent confrontations between the Hutu and Tutsi continue to occur.

Farm women in the crowded Gitega region receive training in improved planting methods from a UN worker.

Burundi and the World

The Republic of Burundi is a small, landlocked country located in east central Africa, between the nations of Rwanda, Zaire, and Tanzania. It is a land of cloud-wrapped mountains, rolling hills, and broad, grassy plateaus, or high plains. Two of its rivers, the Kagera and the Ruvuvu, are the southernmost sources of Egypt's mighty Nile River. Lake Tanganyika, on Burundi's southwest border, is one of the world's largest and loveliest lakes. With spectacular scenery and a warm but comfortable climate, Burundi was once one of Africa's most beautiful and fertile regions. Before the late 19th century, it had a stable government, and its people developed great skill in the arts, especially singing, dancing, and drumming. Today, however, Burundi's problems are among the most serious in the world.

Like many African countries, Burundi has a long history but became an independent nation quite recently. And like many of the younger countries in Africa and other parts of the world, Burundi is considered a developing nation—that is, a nation in which the health, education, and income of the people lag far behind those of people who live in the United States or the nations of Western Europe. Burundi is one of the world's most troubled nations today for four reasons in particular: overcrowding, poverty, violent conflict between two rival peoples, and the lack of a stable government.

Burundi covers an area of 10,759 square miles (28,188 square kilometers), making it about the size of the state of Maryland in the United States. It has a population of 4,989,000, or about 464 people per square mile (177 per square kilometer). This population density makes Burundi one of the most crowded countries in Africa. Although several other nations—and even the state of Maryland—have population densities that are as high as Burundi's, much of their population is concentrated in large cities. In Burundi, on the other hand, only eight percent of the people live in towns or cities. The capital city, Bujumbura, has 272,600 residents, but there are no other large cities. The countryside supports the population, and its resources are desperately strained.

Farming is Burundi's principal source of income. About 92 percent of all Burundians are farmers. Most of them grow food crops to feed their families, or perhaps to trade for cloth and other goods in rural marketplaces. Other farmers grow coffee, cotton, tea, or tobacco to sell for cash. These cash crops are Burundi's only products for export, or sale to other nations. But because most Burundians use ancient farming techniques, and because erosion and centuries of cultivation have worn out the country's soil, Burundi's farms are not very productive. Farmers who grow food crops often have difficulty feeding their families, and the export of cash crops does not produce enough income to pay for the petroleum products, machinery, and other goods that Burundi must import from other countries.

For every U.S. dollar's worth of goods that it exports, Burundi imports more than two dollars' worth of goods. As a result, Burundi has international debts of more than $415 million. According to the United Nations, it is one of the world's 20 poorest countries. In 1981, the last year for which a figure is available, the average per-person annual income of the Burundians was U.S. $200—one of the lowest in the world.

Underlying every aspect of life in Burundi is a centuries-old hatred between two tribal groups called the Hutu and the Tutsi. The Hutu, who are farmers by tradition, established agricultural communities and small kingdoms in the region between the 7th and the 14th centuries. Beginning in the 15th century, groups of cattle-herding nomads, or wanderers, called the Tutsi began migrating from the north into Burundi and the neighboring country of Rwanda. Although the Hutu greatly outnumbered the Tutsi, the larger and more warlike Tutsi soon dominated the Hutu. The Hutu were reduced to the status of serfs, or servants bound by law to the Tutsi-owned land. The Tutsi developed an elaborate social structure, with the Hutu at the bottom and the Tutsi *bami*, or kings, at the top.

Outside forces took control of Burundi's destiny in the 19th century. In 1885, Burundi became a colony of Germany. Thirty years later, when World War I spread to the African colonies of the European powers, Belgium gained control of Germany's territories in East Africa, including Burundi. After the war, Belgium continued to control Burundi, as well as Rwanda. But both the Germans and the Belgians left the Tutsi bami on their throne and left the structure of Burundi's society much as they had found it. As a result, the great gulf between the poor but numerous Hutu and the rich and powerful but much less numerous Tutsi kept widening.

In the years following World War II, liberation movements swept across the African continent like wildfire through the dry savanna. Colony after colony demanded freedom and independence, sometimes violently. Unlike the people of many African nations, the Burundians did not have to fight a war against their European overlords to win their independence. Belgium and the United Nations agreed to make the country independent in 1962.

The achievement of independence did not unite the peoples of Burundi. The Tutsi remained in power in the new government—but the Hutu were increasingly aware of tribal struggles for liberation and equality in other African nations. Right next door in Rwanda, for example, the Hutu majority had managed to seize control from the Tutsi. In Rwanda, the Hutu had political power, and many Tutsi were forced to flee from the country. Most of them came to Burundi, where they increased the strength of the Tutsi group and added to the resentment felt by the Hutu.

In the streets of Bujumbura,
traditional tribal drums beat out the
news of independence on July 1, 1962.

Violence erupted in the late 1960s, when the Tutsi government of Burundi began arresting Hutu leaders. The confrontation continued into the early 1970s. By 1972, civil war had broken out around the country. Hutu uprisings, in which 10,000 or more Tutsi were killed, led to savage massacres of the Hutu by the Tutsi military. The killing on both sides went on for more than a year. At the end of that time, at least 100,000 Hutu had been killed, and more than

85,000 others had fled to Tanzania, Zaire, or Rwanda. Similar fighting and massacres broke out in the summer of 1988. The Tutsi rulers
have been accused of attempted genocide—that is, of trying to wipe
out the entire race of Hutu. Nonetheless, the Hutu still greatly out-
number the Tutsi.

Today, the Tutsi make up 13 percent of Burundi's population.
They control most of the country's limited wealth and nearly all of
the high-ranking positions in the government and in the National
Progress and Unity party (UPRONA), which is the only political party
allowed by law in Burundi. The Hutu, who make up 83 percent of
the population, have little voice in the administration of the country.
Violent confrontations between the two peoples—incidents of rebel-

Hutu victims of the 1972 violence huddle in a refugee camp in Zaire.

lion or discrimination—still occur, and unity between Hutu and Tutsi seems as far away as ever.

The fourth thing that contributes to Burundi's troubles is its lack of a stable government. In 1961, just months before Burundi became independent, the country's first elected prime minister was assassinated after only two weeks in office; the history of high office in Burundi since that time has been one of violence and sudden reversals. Four men have ruled the country since 1966. Each of them arrived at power through a coup d'état—a sudden, violent overthrow of the government, often by the military, which then places an officer in control of the new government.

The most recent coup took place in 1987, when Major Pierre Buyoya overthrew President Jean-Baptiste Bagaza, who had ruled Burundi since leading his own coup in 1976. Buyoya promptly suspended the constitution and dismissed the legislature. He turned the running of the country over to 31 fellow officers, who formed a group called the Military Committee for National Salvation. The committee elected Buyoya president.

It is impossible to predict the course of Burundi's political future, but Buyoya's UPRONA is unlikely either to improve conditions for the Hutu or to allow other political parties to express their ideas. According to Buyoya, however, UPRONA is trying to improve education and health care, to introduce industry and more productive farming methods, and to maintain good relations with other African and world nations that can help Burundi with foreign aid and trade. Burundi's desperate problems cannot be solved overnight, but perhaps—if the Hutu and the Tutsi can work on them together—they can be solved.

The capital city of Bujumbura lies in a sheltered spot at the foot of rugged hills. Much of Burundi's landscape consists of steep, hilly terrain.

A High Land

Burundi is shaped something like a spearhead embedded in east central Africa and aimed southward. To the north, it is bordered by Rwanda, with which it once was united as a German colony. The Akanyaru and Kagera rivers form much of this border. To the east, Burundi is bordered by Tanzania; the Malagarasi River forms part of this border in the southeast. The south—the point of the spearhead—is also bordered by Tanzania, whose territory extends into the waters of Lake Tanganyika. To the southwest, the border between Burundi and Zaire runs down the middle of the lake. To the northwest, the Ruzizi River forms the border between Burundi and Zaire; this river flows from Lake Kivu, in Rwanda.

High and hilly, Burundi lies well above sea level. The highest region is a ridge of mountains that runs north-south through the western part of the country. These mountains have no name, but they are sometimes called the Congo-Nile Crest, or the Congo-Nile Divide, because they divide central Africa into two great basins: Rivers and streams west of the crest flow into the great basin of the Congo River, while those east of the crest flow northward into the Nile River. The highest point in Burundi is located on the crest, northeast of the capital city of Bujumbura; it is 9,055 feet (2,760 meters) above sea level.

East of the Congo-Nile Crest, the land falls away into a huge central plateau, flat in many places but broken by ranges of hills or by steep, sloping cliffs called escarpments. The valleys between the hills and cliffs tend to be swampy. Most of the central plateau, however, consists of grassy plains called savannas or of farmland. The average height above sea level of this part of the country is 5,600 feet (1,700 meters). In the south and southeast, the plateau is a bit lower—about 4,600 feet (1,400 meters) above sea level.

In an effort to combat the ravages of deforestation, workers plant seedlings (below) and tend young saplings on tree farms (facing page). Unfortunately, reforestation programs have had limited success.

The lowest-lying part of Burundi is called the Ruzizi Plain. It is located in the northwest and forms a narrow strip between the Ruzizi River and the Congo-Nile Crest, north of Lake Tanganyika. Bujumbura, the capital, is located where the northeastern tip of the lake meets the southern tip of the Ruzizi Plain. The Ruzizi Plain is about 2,600 feet (800 meters) above sea level. It is part of the enormous system of valleys, gorges, and lakes that is known as the Great Rift Valley. The Great Rift Valley stretches from the Near East to southeastern Africa. It was formed when the plates that form the earth's surface were slowly pulled apart over millions of years. The Red Sea fills part of the Great Rift Valley; so does Lake Tanganyika.

Lake Tanganyika is by far the largest of Burundi's three large lakes. Surrounded by cliffs and forested hills, it is the longest freshwater lake in the world—420 miles (676 kilometers) from north to south. It is also the second-deepest freshwater lake, with a maximum depth of 4,708 feet (1,412 meters); only Lake Baikal, in the Soviet Union, is deeper. Burundi claims very little of Lake Tanganyika—about half of the northern fifth of the lake. The rest belongs to Zaire, Tanzania, and Zambia. Still, the lake provides Burundi with a small but important fishing industry and with some scenic lakeside locations that might someday be developed as tourist resorts.

The country's other major lakes are Lake Cohoha and Lake Rweru. Both are located in the far north, on the border between Burundi and Rwanda. Together with Burundi's portion of Lake Tanganyika, they account for seven percent of Burundi's total area.

Climate and Weather

Although it is located in the world's tropical zone, Burundi does not have the torrid weather that usually is associated with the tropics. It is near the equator, but its altitude—its height above sea level—keeps it from being as hot as, for example, the lowland jungle of nearby Zaire. Burundi's highest areas, along the Congo-Nile Crest, are also the coolest areas. They have an annual average temperature of 57° Fahrenheit (14° centigrade). On the central plateau, which is somewhat lower, the average annual temperature is 68° F (20° C). The lowest part of the country, the Ruzizi Plain, is also the hottest; Bujumbura has an average annual temperature of 77° F (25° C).

Temperatures vary from region to region within the country, and they also vary at different hours of the day. But they do not vary greatly by season. Instead, the seasons in Burundi are determined by rainfall. The country has four seasons: the long wet season (from February to May), the long dry season (from June to August), the short wet season (from September to November), and the short dry season (from December to January).

Most of the country receives from 51 to 63 inches (130 to 160 centimeters) of rainfall a year. Rainfall is heaviest in the northwest and lightest in the northeast. The Ruzizi Plain receives only from 30 to 40 inches (75 to 100 centimeters) a year. In addition, rainfall varies considerably from year to year. Floods are quite rare, but droughts—long periods when rainfall is either entirely absent or far below normal levels—occur once every decade or so.

Plant and Animal Life

Centuries ago, when groups of hunters called the Twa were the only inhabitants of Burundi, majestic forests of towering hardwood trees and flowering shrubs covered much of the land. Each group of new-comers to arrive in Burundi since then has taken more land away from the forests.

The Hutu cleared patches of land for growing food crops. Later, the Tutsi brought their huge herds of cattle, and more land was cleared for grazing. Even without human help, over many years cattle can turn woodland into pasture simply by eating the flowers, shrubs, and small trees. Throughout the centuries of Tutsi dominance, forest gave way to open grassland. Later still came the European colonial administrators, who wanted their colony in Burundi to bring in money. They introduced cash crops, and the establishment of coffee, cotton, and tea plantations meant that trees had to be cleared on a grand scale.

The colonial era has ended, but Burundi's large and growing population and its need to produce cash crops continue to put a terrible strain on the land. Burundi is one of the most deforested countries in tropical Africa. Only two and a half percent of its area contains forest, and the trees that remain are mostly small, scrubby

Although wild animals are now rare in most parts of Burundi, the lakes and rivers remain a sanctuary for many species, some of which are found nowhere else on earth.

trees, such as eucalyptus and acacia. Fig trees are common, and oil palms are found along the shore of Lake Tanganyika.

Deforestation leads to another serious problem: erosion. Burundi's soil, once remarkably fertile, is of poor quality today because, without forests to help hold it in place, much topsoil has been washed away over the years. Reforestation programs aimed at planting young trees where they are most needed have been in operation since the 1940s, but they have not been very successful, because cattle eat many of the newly planted saplings, or the people use them

for fuel. Recently, government programs have had some success planting shrubs and hedges along fields to help control erosion. In general, the soil is more fertile in the east, where there is less drainage down steep hillsides.

Wildlife was once abundant in Burundi. With the destruction of the forests, however, many creatures lost their habitat. Today, forest-dwelling animals such as the elephant, wild boar, and flying lemur are extremely rare and are found only in the few remaining forested areas, mostly in the mountains. Chimpanzees used to live in the forests along the shores of Lake Tanganyika, but their numbers have dwindled and they may have vanished from the region. Even savanna dwellers such as the lion and antelope are scarce, because the swelling population of people and cattle has driven them off the plains. A few hippopotamuses remain in Burundi's rivers and lakes, which also are home to many crocodiles. The rare West African sharp-snouted crocodile used to be found in Lake Tanganyika, but none has been seen in Burundi's waters for many years. Rodents, lizards, snakes, and frogs, however, remain plentiful.

The larger wildlife species are vanishing from the land, but Lake Tanganyika is still rich in fish. The Nile perch, the freshwater sardine, and the *daaga*, a small fish like a whitebait, are the most common food species. Most of the lake's 133 species of fish are endemic in biological terms, meaning that they live only there.

Birds have always been the most varied form of wildlife in Burundi. At least 594 species of birds have been sighted there, ranging from small, jewel-colored honey eaters to the huge vultures that feed on dead animals. Birds that are hunted for food include guinea fowl, ducks, geese, partridges, quail, and snipe. Some of Burundi's bird species—including the redheaded passat, the petilla, and several types of weather birds—are endemic also. Crowned cranes are common, although they are becoming less so as the human population increases.

Burundi also has spiders, termites, ants, flies, and beetles. Several insects are noteworthy because of the health problems that they cause. The anopheles, a type of mosquito, infects humans with malaria, an often fatal disease that causes repeated episodes of high fever and weakness. It is most common along the Ruzizi River. Many people in the same region fall victim to schistosomiasis (also called bilharziasis), a disease that is spread by parasitic worms in the water supply. Another troublesome insect is the tsetse fly. It carries the disease trypanosomiasis, sometimes called sleeping sickness because it afflicts its victims with uncontrollable drowsiness. Sleeping sickness is often found in cattle, and it can infect an entire herd within days. Some cattle may survive, but most human victims die.

The wildlife and environment of Burundi have paid a high price for the growth in the human population during the past century or so. Deforestation, erosion, extinction of species, and the loss of wildlife are problems in many African countries that have experienced similar population growth combined with poverty. Yet Burundi lags behind most other African nations in protective measures. It has no national parks and no wildlife sanctuaries. Some wildlife species are protected by law, but poaching (illegal hunting) is common, and the laws against poaching are almost never enforced. Similarly, the law requires people to obtain permits from the government before cutting trees for fuel, but this law is seldom followed.

It is difficult for people who suffer severe poverty and malnutrition, or who have a tradition of hunting for game, to understand that wildlife and forests are resources that must be safeguarded. But experts in conservation and wildlife biology say that if Burundi does not soon take strong measures to protect its environment and its animals, these resources will be destroyed by the end of the century.

Newspaperman and explorer Henry Morton Stanley was one of the first Europeans to penetrate the mysterious regions around Lake Tanganyika, including the area that later became Burundi.

Early History

The earliest known inhabitants of Burundi were the Twa people. The Twa were related to the Pygmies of the Congo River basin. Short, slender, and brown-skinned, they hunted game and gathered berries and other food in the forests. They lived in groups of four to six families who roamed the forests together, and the only domestic animals they possessed were hunting dogs.

Starting around the 7th century A.D., a new people began migrating into Burundi from the west. The ancestors of these people came from western Africa. They spoke languages that belonged to the widespread Bantu language family. The Bantu migrations eventually carried Bantu peoples into almost every part of Africa south of the Sahara Desert. Those who settled in what is now Burundi called themselves the Hutu. The Hutu were basically peaceful people, farmers who settled on land where they could grow their crops of sorghum (a type of grain), yams, corn, and other vegetables. Some of the Hutu also fished for their food, taking advantage of Burundi's rivers and the enormous freshwater lake, Lake Tanganyika, in the southwestern region. They also introduced metalworking and pottery making. The Hutu outnumbered the Twa and dominated them easily.

Some intermarriage occurred, but most of the Twa retreated into the deep forests to pursue their ancient way of life.

Until the 15th century, the Hutu farmed the land, with kings called *bahinza* ("those who cause things to grow") ruling over local regions. The Hutu organized themselves in groups, or clans, whose members were related to each other. These family groups fell under the jurisdiction of the bahinza.

A second wave of migrations brought more newcomers to Burundi in the 15th and 16th centuries. These were the Tutsi people, often called the Watusi. They originated in the Nile regions to the north and east, in Sudan and Ethiopia, and they came south in search of pastureland. The Tutsi were a tall, warlike people who tended herds of cattle in which they took great pride. Their long-horned cattle were a form of wealth, like money: The more cattle a person owned, the more power and prestige he commanded.

Despite the presence of many more Hutu than Tutsi in Burundi, the Tutsi were able to establish themselves as the ruling class. They made it quite clear that they felt farming was an inferior occupation to cattle herding. Their cows impressed the Hutu with their long horns and the reverence they commanded from the Tutsi herders. It was not long before the Hutu came to prize the cattle as highly as the Tutsi did. Some historians have suggested that the Hutu were

Tutsi boys were trained in dancing, storytelling, and fighting.

Powerful Tutsi princes, called ganwa, *often rebelled against the* mwami's *rule.*

led to believe that Tutsi dominance over them was fated to happen; belief in fate remains fairly strong among the Hutu today.

Whatever the reason, the Hutu soon became serfs, as their agricultural kingdoms gave way to a complex feudal system devised by the Tutsi. In exchange for the prized cattle, they gave away their landholdings and lived on Tutsi land, tilling the soil for their Tutsi patrons and for their own families' needs as well. In return, the Tutsi gave the Hutu military protection against enemies—and the Hutu were reminded of the Tutsi's superior fighting skills.

The system that bound the Hutu to the Tutsi is called cattle clientage. The cattle that the Hutu received from the Tutsi were theirs to care for, not really to own. The cattle, like the Hutu, belonged to the land, which belonged to the Tutsi. The cattle represented the bond between the Tutsi patron and the Hutu client; the contract binding Hutu to Tutsi was called *ubugabire.*

The Tutsi maintained a strict hierarchy, with the king—called the *mwami*—at the top. In theory, the mwami ruled the whole country, the Kingdom of Burundi. Ranked under the mwami, however, were Tutsi princes of royal blood called *ganwa*, who were very powerful within their own domains. In many ways, the situation in Burundi was comparable to the feudal system of medieval Europe. The Hutu were serfs in relation to their Tutsi lords. Like lords, the ganwa ruled over fiefdoms and competed with other ganwa for power. The mwami did his best to keep the ganwa in check, because he did not want any one of them to become so powerful as to threaten his kingship.

Some Hutu, and even some Twa, attained prestige through acts of special bravery or honor. They rose to the Tutsi class. On the other hand, Tutsi who became poor or fell out of favor with the mwami could be reduced to the level of Hutu. But despite these rare cases of movement between classes, the Hutu and the Tutsi remained sharply divided in terms of social standing. Over time, though, they developed a common language, called Kirundi.

Kings and Colonialists

The Tutsi monarchies began with the first mwami, Ntare I Rushatsi, who came to power sometime in the mid-16th century. He was a notable warrior and a shrewd politician who was able to unite the country under a single ruler by a combination of force and diplomacy. Four dynasties, or bloodlines, of kings ruled Burundi. In order, they were the Ntare, the Mwezi, the Mutaga, and the Mwambutsa. Their descendants are known—in the same order—as the Batare, the Bezi, the Bataga, and the Bambutsu. The ganwa clans vied continually for power, and the mwami, who wanted to strengthen his position against the ganwa, developed close ties with some Hutu subchiefs; he hired them to oversee some of his lands. Because of this Hutu-Tutsi collaboration, there may have been more intermarriage and less division between the Hutu and Tutsi in Burundi than in its neighbor, Rwanda, where the Hutu and Tutsi were more deeply divided.

Hidden in the heart of a huge continent, encircled by deep lakes, rivers, and mountains, Burundi had little contact with the outside world. The Arab slave traders who pillaged Kenya and Tanzania after about the 12th century seldom ventured up into Burundi's hills and high plateaus. But in the 19th century, a new presence from the outside world entered the heart of Africa.

Europeans had visited Africa for centuries. Explorers, fortune hunters, slave traders, and colonists from Great Britain, France, Portugal, and other countries had made many parts of Africa their own by the middle of the 19th century. At that point, the world's attention turned to the long-isolated regions of the interior, and Europeans and Americans began to penetrate these hidden lands.

A missionary as well as an explorer, David Livingstone made the first map of the Ruzizi Plain.

Some were explorers, trying to solve the greatest geographical mystery of the time—the source of the Nile. Others wanted to claim colonies for their home countries or hoped to find gold and diamonds. Others still were missionaries, determined that Christianity and empire building should go hand in hand. Three hundred years or so after Ntare I Rushatsi mounted the throne of his highland kingdom, the first of these outsiders reached Burundi.

Mwami Mwezi IV Gisabo sat on the throne when two British explorers, Richard Burton and John Hanning Speke, visited the northern tip of Lake Tanganyika in 1858. They landed at the site of present-day Bujumbura, but their stay in Burundi was brief. They pushed on in search of the Nile's source and eventually discovered Lake Victoria, Africa's largest lake. In 1871, newspaperman Henry Morton Stanley and missionary David Livingstone explored the Ruzizi River and the surrounding plain.

For the most part, however, Burundi remained unvisited by whites. In 1884 and 1885, an international conference was held in Berlin to enable the nations of Europe to settle their conflicting claims to African territory. The Berlin conference granted permission to Germany to control Burundi and the neighboring kingdom of Rwanda. In the early 1890s, German explorers Oskar Baumann and Count von Götzen led expeditions into the area. They made maps and established Germany's territorial claim. Von Götzen later became governor of German East Africa, which was what the Germans were to name this region.

In order to establish control, the Germans made a deal with Mwami Gisabo. They agreed to help him overpower his enemies among the ambitious ganwa, and he agreed to do what they told him to do. By 1907, they had subdued all of the ganwa who had opposed the mwami—or the Germans. The mwami was a puppet king.

By 1908, when this picture was taken, Mwami Gisabo was king in name only.

Mwami Gisabo was succeeded by a 15-year-old boy, Mwami Mutaga IV. Under his rule, the kingship grew even weaker. The ganwa and lesser chiefs took advantage of their mwami's inexperience and youth to regain some of their power. The Germans did not really care, as long as their claim to overlordship was not threatened.

The year 1898 saw the arrival of the first Roman Catholic missionaries in Burundi. Before long, many missions—some of them with schools and hospitals—had been built. But because they found no gold or diamonds for immediate exploitation, the Germans did little in Burundi beyond encouraging the missionary movement. They sent no colonists and few administrators, and they built no railways, roads, or other improvements. Germany's long-term plans for the region called for the establishment of agricultural plantations, but World War I caused those plans to be canceled.

A mission at Muyaga, in eastern Burundi, was one of many that were founded by Roman Catholics in the early 1900s.

The war in Europe spread to the European colonies in Africa, and Germany completely lost control of German East Africa. Belgian troops entered Burundi and met relatively little resistance from the German officers and their small force of 1,400 African troops. By June 27, 1916, Belgium controlled Burundi.

After the war, in 1923, the League of Nations—the forerunner of the United Nations—assigned Rwanda and Burundi to Belgium as a single territory called Ruanda-Urundi. Although they were lumped together by the colonial authorities and then by the League of Nations, Rwanda and Burundi had always been separate countries. They had shared the same mix of Hutu and Tutsi peoples and the same system of ubugabire, but they had never come under one ruler.

During the years under Belgian authority, the mwami of Burundi retained his kingship, but Africans were allowed little part in government. Many Burundians were taken to work in mines in the Belgian colony of the Congo (now called Zaire), west of Burundi. Present-day historians have criticized the Belgians for their indifference to developing Burundi's economy and for their refusal to grant civil rights to the Africans during the nearly 40 years that they remained in authority. The Belgians focused more of their energy on the Congo, where mining was extremely profitable.

The Belgians did, however, work to establish an educational system. Through the schools French became established as the second language of Burundi. They also introduced large-scale farming of cash crops such as coffee. Although the Belgians, and not the African workers, reaped the profits from these products, the cash crops did provide Burundi with the basis for an economy that could include exports and international trade. In 1946, at the conclusion of World War II, the United Nations made Ruanda-Urundi a UN trust territory. It directed Belgium to help Ruanda-Urundi develop politically so that its people could govern themselves. Belgian diplomats helped Burundians form political parties, with the understanding that independence would be the outcome.

Accompanied by a Belgian officer, Mwami Mwambutsa IV and his wife leave church on the eve of their nation's independence. Mwambutsa was dethroned four years later.

Independence and Government

The 1950s were a time of transition between old ways and new ways. Nearly all Burundians had lived their whole life in a colony—first of Germany, then of Belgium. Only a few very old people remembered a time when their kingdom was free and cut off from the outside world. Now, with the support of the United Nations, it was moving toward freedom once again.

Some aspects of life in Burundi, however, were slow to change. One such aspect was the Tutsi overlordship of the Hutu. During the 1950s, some Hutu—often those who had been influenced by the belief in human equality that the Christian missionaries preached—began to feel that the old system of Tutsi domination should be discarded. They wanted the Hutu to share equally with the Tutsi in the coming independence. In 1955, with help from the Belgian administrators, the Hutu made proposals for ending the feudal system of ubugabire and for redistributing the Tutsi-owned land. But the Tutsi had no intention of giving up the power and wealth they had maintained over centuries. Confronted with the restlessness of the Hutu, the feuding Tutsi ganwa forgot their differences and united to protect their traditional way of life. The Hutu were unable to get

Louis Rwagasore was the crown prince, a party leader, and Burundi's first prime minister. Assassination ended his career.

their proposals made into law; not until 1977, 15 years after independence, was the ubugabire contract abolished.

The 1950s also saw the birth and growth of political parties as the Burundians, aided by the Belgians, prepared for self-government. The National Progress and Unity party (UPRONA) was founded in 1958 by Ganwa Louis Rwagasore, son of Mwami Mwambutsa IV. The Tutsi nobility, chiefs, and army flocked to this party. The Hutu formed several parties, but these parties were considerably weaker than UPRONA because they contained no chiefs, nobles, or members of the traditional government. The largest of them was called the People's party (PP); it later merged with a small group of UPRONA members who favored equality between the two peoples. Another early Hutu organization was called the Christian Democratic party.

Belgium supervised Burundi's first elections, which were held in September 1961. The chief purpose of the elections was to choose a prime minister to head the government so that independence could be granted. The people also elected 64 representatives to a legislature called the National Assembly. The elections were a sweeping victory for UPRONA, which won most of the seats in the National Assembly. Louis Rwagasore was elected prime minister. Just a few weeks later, though, he was assassinated. His brother-in-law, a Tutsi ganwa named André Muhirwa, became prime minister in his place. As for the assassination, two leaders of the Christian Democratic party were arrested, convicted, and executed for the crime.

Having cast her vote in Burundi's first elections, a woman leaves a polling station.

One week before Independence Day in 1962, the departure lounge of Bujumbura Airport was crowded with white Europeans leaving the country.

The United Nations had always hoped that Ruanda-Urundi would become independent as a single united nation. This would give the advantage of increased territory and resources, and it seemed reasonable because both kingdoms had the same ethnic peoples and a common language. But neither the Rwandans nor the Burundians favored joining their destinies. By now, Rwanda was controlled by the Hutu, who had eliminated the kingship and wanted to establish a republic. The dominant Tutsi of Burundi, on the other hand, planned to preserve the post of mwami and become independent as a kingdom. The mwami's role would be one of ceremony only, as the country would be governed by the prime minister and the National Assembly, but the Burundians thought that it should be retained. On June 27, 1962, therefore, the United Nations General Assembly voted to allow the trust territory of Ruanda-Urundi to become two independent nations, the Republic of Rwanda and the Kingdom of Burundi.

An Independent Kingdom

Burundi officially became independent on July 1, 1962. Its head of state was Mwami Mwambutsa IV, and its head of government was Prime Minister Muhirwa. Unfortunately, the nation's first prime minister proved to be a weak statesman who was unable to keep his government together. Tutsi ganwa and military officers began seeking power, plotting and feuding much as they had done in earlier years. In 1966, four years after independence, Mwami Mwambutsa IV was dethroned after more than 50 years as king. Aided by a group of ambitious officers, the mwami's son and heir seized the throne and declared himself Mwami Ntare V. He named the leader of the officers, Captain Michel Micombero, his prime minister.

While Ntare (left) paid a state visit to Congolese president Joseph Mobutu, his one-time allies at home seized power and ended his kingship.

The usurper's reign was a short one. Just two months later, he was overthrown in turn. Micombero, who had helped Ntare V get rid of his father, now decided to get rid of Ntare. He and his followers seized control of the government, declared that the kingship was abolished, and renamed the country the Republic of Burundi. After 400 years, the reign of the mwami of Burundi was over.

Micombero ruled Burundi for the next decade. At first he took the title president, but in 1972 he gave himself the combined titles of president and prime minister. Then, in 1974, he introduced a new constitution that made UPRONA the only political party allowed by law in the country; the PP and the remnants of the Christian Democratic party were disbanded. Furthermore, the constitution made UPRONA itself the official sovereign, or head of state. But as UPRONA's secretary-general, holder of the highest post in the party, Micombero kept a firm hold on the reins of power.

Two Peoples at War

The years of Micombero's rule widened the gap between Tutsi and Hutu. Micombero was, of course, a Tutsi, and unlike some of his fellow tribespeople he was utterly opposed to any sort of agreement, equality, or partnership between the two peoples. The Hutu had no voice in government, and their dissatisfaction increased. In 1969, Micombero arrested 30 of the most prominent and successful Hutu businessmen in Bujumbura, claiming that they had tried to overthrow the government. Again, in 1971, the Hutu were believed to be behind a coup attempt. Some Hutu leaders were jailed. The following year, the violence that had been brewing for many years erupted.

In April 1972, the Hutu launched their strongest uprising against the Micombero government. Many thousands of Hutu took up arms and killed some 10,000 Tutsi, including Ntare V, their former mwami. The coup attempt failed, however; the Hutu were

(continued on p. 57)

SCENES OF
BURUNDI

◄ *Birds are the most varied form of wildlife in Burundi. Naturalists have sighted nearly 600 species there.*

➤ *Lions are increasingly scarce on the savannas, as growing populations of both people and cattle encroach upon their habitat.*

⌄ *Burundi's rivers and lakes continue to provide a home for a small number of hippopotamuses.*

▾ *Poaching and deforestation have combined to reduce Burundi's once abundant herds of elephants.*

➤ Coffee remains Burundi's main cash crop, although tea production has increased in recent years. The highland hills are dotted with plantations of both crops.

⋎ Herds of zebras and antelope sweep across the plains of the Ruvuvu river basin.

▾ *Traditional boats rest on the shores of Lake Tanganyika.*

▲ Burundi claims the northern one-tenth of Lake
Tanganyika, the world's longest and second-deepest
freshwater lake. Lakes Rweru and Cohoha, in the
northeastern part of Burundi, are sometimes called the
bird lakes because of wildfowl found there.

➤ More than 90 percent of Burundi's population is
engaged in farming. The combination of a growing
population and deteriorating soil quality has prompted
the government to sponsor many public works projects
designed to increase agricultural productivity.

⋏ *Young Burundians pose outside their home. Tin-roofed huts such as these are a common sight throughout the countryside.*

▲ *The Palace of the Nation is located in Bujumbura, as are embassies, courts of law, government offices, the airport, and the national university. Bujumbura is also the hub of banking and industry.*

▼ *In Kirundi and French, this stone slab commemorates the independence of Burundi, achieved on July 1, 1962.*

(continued from p. 48)

Michel Micombero quashed several bloody Hutu uprisings only to be overthrown by members of his own party.

unable to dislodge Micombero from power. The enraged Tutsi retaliated by slaughtering at least 100,000 Hutu in the months following the coup attempt. Whole villages were wiped out, and entire rural districts were reduced to smoking rubble.

The Hutu fought back in many parts of the country, attacking and killing the Tutsi whenever they could, but the Tutsi had automatic rifles and hand grenades, while the Hutu guerrillas had few guns and little military skill. As the fighting raged on, reaching the level of a civil war, the Tutsi kept the upper hand. Many more Hutu than Tutsi were killed. Thousands more Hutu fled for their lives, clutching their few possessions, to neighboring countries. In July 1973, a little more than a year after the civil war broke out, the United Nations high commissioner for refugees estimated that there were at least 40,000 Hutu refugees from Burundi in Tanzania, 35,000 in Zaire, and 10,000 in Rwanda. Some Hutu guerrilla bands escaped to Tanzania and Rwanda but continued to make raids across the border into Burundi. Micombero's troops attacked the rebels in the border regions and protested to the Tanzanian and Rwandan governments. As a result, Burundi's relations with these two nations were poor.

By the end of 1973, Micombero's government had restored order. The Hutu uprising was over. But the uprising and the savage suppression that followed it had increased the hatred, fear, and mistrust between the Hutu and the Tutsi. The civil war had also given the Tutsi an opportunity to make sure that they would stay in power for some time to come. During the violence, Tutsi forces had systematically sought out and killed the educated individuals among the Hutu. They had eliminated those who held technical and professional jobs, those who had attended college or traveled abroad, and

even those who could merely read and write. The Tutsi hoped by these measures to eliminate any potential Hutu leaders who might stir up renewed political unrest. As a result of this selective killing, the Hutu were left not only terrified but also leaderless. Although new leaders have arisen among them, and although hostility between the two peoples continues to be strongly felt on both sides, the Hutu have remained a subordinate people since the failure of their revolt. Their resistance to Tutsi domination today is scattered, not organized.

Savage massacres by the Tutsi after the Hutu uprising in 1972 ended in capture (left) and death (below) for hundreds of thousands of Hutu.

Two New Coups

Having put down the Hutu rebellion, Micombero turned his attention to party politics. In 1974, members of UPRONA elected their secretary-general to the presidency of the country for another seven years. Micombero was not destined, however, to serve out his term. In November 1976, a group of army officers who were impatient with his rule took matters into their own hands. In a swift coup, they overthrew Micombero and sent him into exile. The officers then organized themselves into a body called the Supreme Revolutionary Council and elected their leader, Lieutenant Colonel Jean-Baptiste Bagaza, president. Lieutenant Colonel Édouard Nzambimana was made prime minister.

The Supreme Revolutionary Council set forth its goals in the Declaration of Fundamental Aims, a document that called for the elimination of dishonest government officials and for the growth of justice and unity throughout the land. Prime Minister Nzambimana announced that these goals would be met by 1981, at which time he would turn over the government to officials elected by the people from the civilian, or nonmilitary, population.

Two years later, Bagaza eliminated the post of prime minister. He did, however, call for a national meeting of UPRONA in 1979. At this meeting, the party created the Central Committee, made up of civilians and headed by President Bagaza, to replace the Supreme Revolutionary Council as the governing body. Bagaza and UPRONA wrote a new constitution, and the Burundians voted to accept it in 1981. Under this constitution, the people were scheduled to vote in 1982 for 52 representatives to the new National Assembly. These elections were held on schedule; all candidates were members of UPRONA. Bagaza was reelected president of UPRONA in July 1982 and president of Burundi in August. In both elections, he was the only candidate.

The change from Micombero's regime to Bagaza's regime did nothing to improve the status or prospects of Burundi's Hutu majority. Hoping to improve the world's opinion of Burundi, Bagaza promised that massacres such as that of 1972 would never happen again, and he invited the Hutu who had fled to return to their homeland. Few of them, however, chose to accept this invitation. At the same time, Bagaza started a policy of harassment and repression against the Roman Catholic church in Burundi, because he felt that some Catholic clergymen were too sympathetic to the Hutu and also that they were spreading information abroad that made Burundi look bad. In 1985, he arrested several priests and the archbishop of Gitega, a city in central Burundi. He also ordered a number of foreign missionaries to leave the country, claiming that they had performed religious services on weekdays—an act that broke a rule made by Bagaza's government. Amnesty International, an international organization whose members investigate violations of human rights around the world, announced that 20 clergymen were being held in Burundi without trial. The government admitted the arrests, then claimed that some of the priests had been released.

The conflict between church and state continued. In 1986, the government took over the administration of many of the country's Roman Catholic seminaries, or religious schools. In 1987, morning prayer meetings were banned. At that point, Bagaza seemed to realize that he had gone too far. His antichurch policies were unpopular even with many of his fellow Tutsi and with UPRONA members. In an attempt to soften his harshness toward the church, he announced that all Catholic priests who were still in jail would be released.

In September 1987, Bagaza went to Canada to attend a conference. While he was away, a group of officers led by Major Pierre Buyoya staged a coup, overthrew the government, and took control of Burundi. Buyoya suspended the 1981 constitution and dismissed the National Assembly. His supporters formed the 31-member Mil-

One day after posing for this photo with Djibouti president Gouled Aptidon (upper left), Canadian prime minister Brian Mulroney (lower left), and French president François Mitterand (lower right) on September 2, 1987, at a summit in Canada, Burundian president Jean-Baptiste Bagaza (upper right) learned his government had been overthrown in a military coup. Bagaza was not seen at the summit the next day.

itary Committee for National Salvation (CMSN). The CMSN promptly elected Buyoya president. It also appointed a dozen or so civilians to the Council of Ministers. UPRONA, many of whose leaders had been friends and supporters of Bagaza, was forbidden to hold meetings or publish its newspapers in the months after the coup, but during 1988 the party was reorganized and became active once again, with Buyoya as its leader.

Former president Bagaza made one attempt to regain power. He tried to return to Burundi in November 1987, but the Buyoya government was able to stop him by the simple method of refusing to give his pilot permission to land at the Bujumbura airfield.

One of the first acts of the Buyoya government was the easing of rules against religious activity; this made some observers think that one reason for the coup might have been anger at Bagaza's harsh treatment of Catholic priests. Buyoya also was careful not to

Father Gabriel Barakana was one of five people convicted in 1985 of sending a letter to their bishop urging defiance of Bagaza's ban on weekday religious services. All were declared prisoners of conscience by Amnesty International in 1986.

include among his ministers any who had served in the Bagaza regime. Despite the fresh start, however, the outlook for most Burundians has not improved. Like all of Burundi's leaders since the 16th century, Buyoya is a Tutsi, and he is not known to be sympathetic to the Hutu. Furthermore, he governs as a military dictator and has not yet restored either the constitution or voting rights to the people of Burundi.

The most important political event in recent years, and Buyoya's biggest challenge, was a Hutu uprising in northern Burundi in August 1988. Angry because military maneuvers in the area had interfered with their profitable practice of smuggling coffee into Rwanda, Hutu farmers attacked Tutsi government workers, doctors, and ranchers. The army reacted swiftly and savagely, killing thousands of Hutu villagers. Estimates of the death toll ranged from 5,000 to 50,000. Buyoya's forces restored control by October, but cooperation and peace between the two peoples seems further out of reach than ever in the aftermath of the killings. In October 1988, Buyoya reintroduced the post of prime minister and filled it with a Hutu, Adrien Sibomana. But the position carries little real power and the Hutu continue to feel that they are excluded from political decision making.

Government and the Military

With the dismissal of the National Assembly, control of lawmaking passed into the hands of the CMSN and the Council of Ministers, both of which are headed by President Buyoya. For purposes of local government, Burundi is divided into 15 provinces. Each province has a capital city, although in many cases these capitals are merely small towns that serve as administrative and market centers for the surrounding rural regions. The provinces are divided into subdivisions called *arrondissements*, which are something like the counties within the states of the United States. The arrondissements are in turn subdivided into communes, or townships. The provinces are administered by governors who are appointed by the president.

Burundi's judicial system was based on a combination of traditional tribal customs and German and French law codes that had been introduced by the Belgians. In 1986, the country had 122 small courts scattered around the arrondissements and a provincial court in each province. Courts of appeals were located in Bujumbura, Gitega, and Ngozi, the three largest cities. The Supreme Court was located in Bujumbura, as were special courts for cases involving trade and labor disputes. It is not known how much of this system remains in force under the Buyoya government.

At the time independence was granted, Burundi had an army and a police force. The two were joined into one force in 1967. Since then, a navy and an air force have been formed. In 1987, the most recent year for which information about the military is available, the armed forces totaled 7,200 men, with 5,500 in the army, 150 in the air force, 50 in the navy, and 1,500 in a special paramilitary commando unit for police action and riot control.

Strife between Tutsi and Hutu is not limited to Burundi. This Tutsi fled to a Burundian refugee camp when the Hutu seized power in neighboring Rwanda.

The People of Burundi

Burundi is populated by four ethnic groups of people—that is, groups whose members are racially or culturally similar. They are the Hutu, the Tutsi, the non-African, and the Twa peoples. Considerable intermixing between the Hutu and the Tutsi has occurred, usually through marriage between Tutsi men and Hutu women. For the most part, however, the two groups remain as clearly separated as they were centuries ago, when the Tutsi herders first entered the realm of the Hutu farmers. The Hutu are the majority, making up 83 percent of the population. The Tutsi account for 13 percent of the population. Non-African residents—Europeans, Arabs, and Asians—total three percent, and the Twa make up one percent. Other Africans living in Burundi include about 70,000 Tutsi refugees from Rwanda and Zaire. Of the non-African population, most of whom live in the capital city of Bujumbura, some 3,000 are Europeans and about 2,000 are Indians and Pakistanis. Many of the Europeans are involved in church-related activities.

The Hutu, the Tutsi, and the Twa are all African, but they differ in physical appearance and in their ways of life. On the average, a Hutu man is 5 feet 5 inches (162.5 centimeters) tall and weighs

Hutu refugees crowded into Zaire when their 1972 coup attempt failed.

about 130 pounds (58.5 kilograms). The Hutu tend to be stocky and muscular.

The Hutu are considered part of the East African Lake Region Bantu tribes. They originally came from the equatorial region in the north. They have long been agriculturalists. Both men and women use hoes to till the ground and plant their many crops. They have passed down their farming methods for many centuries, planting different crops at different times of the year so as to reap the maximum benefits from the soil and the changing seasons. For example, October and November are good months in which to plant corn, millet, and beans, because the long dry season ends in August. In January, when beans are harvested, sorghum is planted. Root crops such as cassava (from which a flour called manioc is made) and yams are planted in February and March.

In the Hutu way of life, hard work is an important virtue. Boys and girls begin helping with chores at around age five; they also are given lessons in the proper way to behave and in the values of their society, which places strong emphasis on family closeness and sharing. Most Hutu are farmers today, although a few have trained for positions in business and government. Since the 1972 fighting, however, the Hutu have been less active in those areas.

Because of their association with Tutsi patrons in centuries past, Hutu are also adept at handling livestock, especially the prized cattle that were introduced to Burundi by the Tutsi. The cows give milk for drinking and to make products such as butter; their dung is used to fertilize fields and, when dried, as a house-building material. The cattle have long symbolized the patron-client relationship between the dominant Tutsi and the subservient Hutu. Hutu feelings about this relationship are reflected in some proverbs about the Tutsi that are less than flattering: for example, "The Tutsi whose sick eyes you cure will open them wide in order to devour you" and "The Tutsi that you lodge in your passageway will take your bed."

The Tutsi, on the other hand, have developed a few sayings of their own that show their disdain for farming and their admiration for cattle herding: "Thou, oh cow, spare me from the fatigue of the hoe" is one Tutsi prayer. Throughout their history, the Tutsi have been pastoralists, or herders, constantly moving to areas where their cattle could find good pasture. Anthropologists (scientists who study human cultures) consider them a Nilotic people—that is, one that

The long-horned Ancholi cattle introduced by the Tutsi are imposing creatures. They impressed the Hutu, who became caretakers of the Tutsi's vast herds.

originated more than 2,000 years ago in the area between the Nile River in the Sudan and the Ethiopian highlands. When they first began moving south into Rwanda and Burundi, they spoke a Nilotic language. Gradually they adopted the Bantu language of the Hutu, called Kirundi.

The Tutsi are well known for their height, angular features, and slender build. The average Tutsi man is 5 feet 8 inches (170 centimeters) tall and weighs about 126 pounds (63 kilograms). Some Tutsi are 6 or even 7 feet (180 or 210 centimeters) tall. It has been customary for male Tutsi youths to receive training in speechmaking, storytelling, social graces, traditional dances, and military skills. At one time, this training was done at the residences of the ganwa or the mwami. On completing the training, the young men were

Dance has long been highly esteemed in Burundi. These dancers performed at the public ceremonies celebrating independence in 1962.

considered members of adult society. The Tutsi traditionally measured their wealth and prosperity in terms of the number and health of their livestock, but they did not kill the cattle for food.

The Twa of Burundi are remnants of the earliest inhabitants of the region. They are related to the short, forest-dwelling Pygmies of Zaire. The Twa are actually larger in stature than Pygmies: The average Twa man is 5 feet 1 inch (152.5 centimeters) tall and weighs about 105 pounds (47 kilograms). Like the Pygmies, the Twa prefer to dwell in the forest. Centuries ago, they retreated deeper and deeper into remote regions as Hutu farmers disturbed the forest. Today, some Twa carry on the hunting-and-gathering way of life of their ancestors in Burundi's few remaining wild areas. Others have become craftspeople and have settled near the Hutu and Tutsi.

The Twa speak Kirundi, but it is slightly different from the Kirundi spoken by the Hutu and Tutsi. The second official language of Burundi is French, which is used in secondary schools, in science, and in government. Swahili is also spoken, mostly along Lake Tanganyika and in Bujumbura. Swahili is a mixture of Arabic and various Bantu languages. It developed as trade between the Arabs and the Africans of the Indian Ocean coast grew between the 12th and the 19th centuries. In East Africa, Swahili is recognized as a useful "trade language," which means it is used in marketplaces and cities when business is being transacted.

A traditional greeting in Kirundi is *"Amashyo,"* or "May you have herds [of cattle]." The person answering back says, *"Amashongore,"* which means "I wish you herds of females." Not surprisingly, Kirundi is filled with references to the virtues of the cow. Speakers of Kirundi use cattle as metaphors for health, happiness, wealth, and prosperity. The words say "I wish you herds," but they mean, "I hope you are well and leading a good life."

The importance of cattle (*inka* in Kirundi) as an object of reverence cannot be overemphasized. The cattle are said to be dedicated

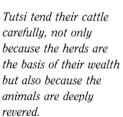

Tutsi tend their cattle carefully, not only because the herds are the basis of their wealth but also because the animals are deeply revered.

to God, whom the Burundians call Imana, so they are carefully tended, prayed to, and treated according to specific customs. Some customs are taboos—that is, rules that forbid certain actions. For example, it is taboo to heat or boil milk because it is feared that such an action would interfere with the cows' milk production. Another taboo forbids drinking milk on the same day that peas or peanuts are eaten. It also is the custom to name each cow. When a cow dies, its meat is eaten (unless it died of disease) and its horns are driven into the ground near the house to bring the family good fortune. The lives of people and cattle are believed to be bound together, so that when the herd is fertile and healthy, its owners will have a good life.

Religion

Traditionally, Burundians have had a strong belief that everything that happens is fated to happen. According to this belief, people cannot change the course of nature or the future but must trust in the goodness of Imana. "Imana is the giver" and "Everything rests in Imana" are sayings that illustrate this way of thinking.

Imana is the supreme source of all goodness and also the life force of all things. The name of Imana appears in all aspects of life. Some children's names are Kaimana (Little Imana), Ndorimana (Appearance of Imana), and Mbonimana (Gift of Imana). The name is also used as an oath: "May Imana give me a stroke," for example, "if I am lying." It is used also in blessings, greetings, and the rites of marriage and death.

The Catholic church began sending missionaries to Burundi in the late 1800s. Protestant missions were established by 1926. By 1969, more than half of the population had converted to some form of Christianity. Today, 78 percent of Burundians are Roman Catholic; 7 percent are Protestant. The only other world religion to make inroads in Burundi is Islam; about one percent of Burundians are Muslim, or followers of Islam. But 40 percent of all Burundians—including many Christians—also have religious beliefs that come from the native tradition. Many of these people still follow aspects of traditional religion that are especially important in their families or clans.

Burundi's traditional beliefs go back hundreds of years. They are a form of animism, which is a belief that certain objects in the physical world, such as trees, stones, or animals, contain spirits that can influence human lives for good or ill.

Respect for ancestors is also an important part of traditional religion. Many Hutu believe that the spirits of deceased ancestors can be malicious and bring misfortune to the family. These families may call in a diviner (fortune-teller, or person believed to communicate with the spirit world) to try and appease the ancestral spirits. The Tutsi, on the other hand, see their relationship with the ancestral spirits as one of reverence rather than fear.

One animist ritual that has been carried on for years is *kubandwa*, a countrywide grain harvest festival. It honors Kiranga, a spirit who is considered to be the leader of all departed ancestors.

Kubandwa is a time when young men paint themselves with special decorations and chant and dance. One of the men appears as Kiranga, carrying a sacred spear. The ceremonies end with a cleansing rite at a stream.

Another traditional ceremony was *umuganuro*, the fertility ceremony. In the days when the mwami was king of Burundi, the Tutsi ganwa and their Hutu clients sealed their ubugabire contracts at this festival. The mwami played an important part in festival rites, at which his sacred drum—the *karyenda*—was played. In an agricultural economy, fertility is a concept of central importance because a good harvest is essential for everyone's survival. At the traditional ceremony of umuganuro, a virgin maiden planted sorghum seed to mark the start of a prosperous, fertile harvest.

Family Life

The umuganuro maiden was a symbol of fertility. Because they can bear children, women are respected, but they have very little authority in decision making. Tradition places much value on a woman's performance of her duties—and foremost among those duties are bearing children and rearing them. Further, if a woman is fertile, it is believed that her fertility will be transmitted into the seeds she plants, so in farming families women do most of the planting.

Children are highly valued, as are motherhood and parenthood in general. One Burundian proverb says, "The greatest sorrow is to have no children to mourn for you." Men take fatherhood very seriously. The proverb "The husband and father is responsible for the family" clearly indicates the role of men in Burundi society. Family ties are very powerful. Concepts such as respect and love for parents and loyalty and trust within the family are taught early in childhood.

It was once common for a Burundian man to have more than one wife. This custom is less common today, because both Christian churches and civil law forbid it, but it still occurs. Traditionally, the father helped find a first wife for his son when the boy was in his late teens or early twenties. Today, the parents of the boy and the potential bride meet to discuss matters. One matter to decide upon is the "bridewealth," which is a gift of goods made by the groom's family to the family of the bride. The bridewealth may consist of cattle, goats, and hoes. More sophisticated Burundians, especially city dwellers, substitute cash, clothing, or furniture.

In a series of meetings, the parents continue to discuss the joining of the families through marriage. When at last they reach agreement, a pot of beer is blessed in the name of the families' ancestors. Drinking beer through straws is important in events such as marriage negotiations. (The Burundians drink beer at all important events, as well as in all social interactions. To refuse beer, in fact, is considered an insult.)

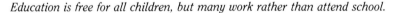

Education is free for all children, but many work rather than attend school.

These huts feature thatched roofs, but shrinking forests have made leaves and fronds scarce. Today, most huts are roofed with tin.

On the day of the wedding, the bridewealth is delivered to the bride's house. The bride receives blessings and a crown of flowers that represents her hope for motherhood. She leaves her home, often tearfully, to join the wedding festivities at her new home. Traditionally, her parents do not attend.

Years ago, Burundian homes were shaped somewhat like beehives and made of grass and mud, with woven leaves for the roof. Today, dried mud and sticks are still used as building materials, but some homes are made of wood or cement blocks. Leaves for the roofs are becoming scarce, so sheets of tin are used instead. Because most of the family's time is spent working or cooking outdoors, the size of the dwelling is kept to a minimum. The family dwellings are surrounded by courtyards, and a group of family homes and their yards will usually be enclosed by a mud and stick wall. In Tutsi tradition, the wives were housed separately; however, Hutu husbands and wives shared the same house.

Most babies are born at home, with the assistance of midwives and other women. Six days after birth, the baby is presented to the family in a ceremony called *ujusohor*. The new mother is greeted with flowers to crown her head, gifts of beer, and sometimes money.

Only after the child is toddling about is it formally given a name. In the *kuvamukiriri*, or naming ceremony, the paternal grandfather gives the child a proper name, a clan name, and a nickname or two. Christian families may also baptize the baby at this time.

One reason that children are not named immediately has to do with the realities of survival. Diseases such as measles and diarrhea take the lives of many babies. Burundi has an infant mortality rate of 134, which means that 134 of every 1,000 babies born die in infancy. Death rates for toddlers and children are also high.

Most children are breast-fed for as long as their mothers have milk, and they see a lot of activity while being carried around on their mothers' back. Later, when they are older, children ride one of their mothers' hips. At age two or three they begin eating the typical Burundian diet of beans, corn, peas, millet, sorghum, cassava, sweet potatoes, and bananas. This diet is starchy, high in carbohydrates, and low in fats and proteins. Meat is eaten rarely and makes up about two percent of the average Burundian's total food intake.

Much work goes into producing meals. Cassava is a root vegetable that must be washed, pounded, and strained to separate the flour from the root fibers. Sorghum, a grain grown for its rounded, starchy seeds, is ground and made into pancakes or porridge.

Combinations of grains and beans or peas, or of corn and beans, provide protein, vitamins, and minerals. Unfortunately, however, protein levels are generally quite low. Many Burundians suffer from a protein-deficiency disease called *kwashiorkor*. This disease is particularly dangerous for children. Those who survive it are likely to have liver damage, stunted growth, and reduced immunity to many troublesome diseases such as dysentery and pneumonia.

Bujumbura is a center for trade and a major market for a wide variety of fruits and vegetables grown on the Ruzizi Plain.

Town and Country

A visitor to Burundi's capital city of Bujumbura might easily hear Kirundi, French, and Swahili all spoken within a few minutes' time. Also, because Bujumbura is the hub of Burundi's international activity, several other languages might be heard as well.

Bujumbura is the largest, most important city in Burundi. It has a population of 272,600, and this figure is expected to increase greatly by the end of the century. Not only is Bujumbura the administrative capital, it is the center of business, trade, industry, transportation, education, medicine, and culture. Situated on the north shore of Lake Tanganyika, it is Burundi's main port for passenger and freight traffic on the lake. Travelers to Burundi inevitably go through Bujumbura, and the city has several hotels, including a modern, international-class hotel that opened during a Franco-African summit meeting in December 1984.

Bujumbura was once called Usumbura. It became the capital while Burundi was under Belgian administration as a UN trust territory called Ruanda-Urundi. European influence is seen in many buildings in the residential and business quarters. Some sections of the city, however, especially *la ville indigène* (French for "the native town") are clearly African and not European at all.

Bujumbura has a population of 272,600 and many hotels and restaurants. Life in the capital presents a sharp contrast to rural life.

Embassies, ministries, and courts of law are located in Bujumbura. The Supreme Court, one of the three courts of appeals, the National Assembly, the national university, as well as important schools and libraries, are all in Bujumbura. As a business center, Bujumbura is home to the Central Bank (Banque de la République de Burundi), four commercial banks, and a development bank. Many commercial, trading, and retail firms are located there.

The most industrialized area of Burundi, the capital city has a cement factory, a brewery, textile and clothing industries, and soap manufacturing facilities. One of the nation's two coffee factories— which together process the entire coffee crop—can be found in Bujumbura; the other is in Gitega. Because coffee is the nation's largest cash crop for export and because it is a seasonal crop, employment rates and the prices of goods in Bujumbura go up and down according to the time of year. That is, during the coffee harvest, many people are employed, and the prices of goods are inflated, or high. After the harvest is sold, at the end of the season, people lose their jobs and the economy declines. This up-and-down pattern occurs every year.

Bujumbura also has a thermoelectric plant for generating power and a wide variety of craftspeople, including tailors and basket weavers. A lively open-air market displays food along with the wares of craftspeople and artists. There the visitor can see handwoven baskets with traditional geometric designs, handworked iron goods, carved

Shops in market towns offer very few imported items. Nevertheless, farmers journey to such towns as Ngozi, Rugari, and Ruyigi for supplies.

wooden items such as walking sticks and canes, woven cloths and fishnets, and much more.

The government hopes to encourage more tourism, which could be a source of income. Recently, a modern international airport—vastly better than the old one—was built in Bujumbura, making Burundi far easier to reach. Eventually, as Bujumbura becomes better known abroad, the city can count on nearby Lake Tanganyika, with its exotic birds such as pelicans, flamingos, and marabou storks, as a tourist attraction.

The capital city is fairly cosmopolitan, because foreigners who live in Burundi tend to be concentrated in Bujumbura. These include diplomatic personnel, educators and researchers, people connected with Catholic and Protestant missions, and merchants. Restaurants are plentiful. While much of the country is eating cassava and sweet potatoes, the urbanites can eat fish caught in Lake Tanganyika. The

Villagers gather around a fountain in the cooperative of Butezi to tell stories, trade news, and refresh themselves.

city is supplied with rice, fruit, and vegetables grown on the nearby Ruzizi Plain. There is a sports center complete with a swimming pool and golf, tennis, racing, and boating facilities—again, the Belgian influence.

Roads connect Bujumbura with Gitega, the second most important city. Gitega lies to the east of Bujumbura, in the center of the country near the Ruvuvu River. For centuries before the Belgian administration, Gitega was the capital of Burundi. Here the mwami held royal court and the ganwa received their training, gathered for traditional ceremonies, and hatched their plots.

Gitega is not a large city compared with most United States cities; its population is about 95,300. But in Burundi, where most people are farmers, Gitega is a good-sized city, and it is growing fast. As recently as 1970, only 5,000 people lived there. Tourists go to Gitega to see a museum that houses the nation's traditional gold artifacts, especially things that belonged to the royal court, and to get a sense of the country's history.

Gitega is located in the highlands, 6,000 feet (1,800 meters) above sea level, in an area that has the nation's highest population density. The climate is well suited to coffee trees and banana trees;

Gitega has one of Burundi's two coffee-processing plants and is the nation's second-largest city. These Burundians carry produce to the market there.

therefore, Gitega is the site of one of the country's two coffee-processing factories and of a new brewery that makes beer from bananas. Tea plantations are found both in Gitega and nearby Muramvya, where a thermoelectric plant supplies power.

Bujumbura and Gitega are the only sizable cities. Ngozi, Rugari, and Karuzi in the north and Ruyigi, Rutana, and Bururi in the south are all market towns where people gather to buy, sell, and trade. Ngozi, with a population of 20,000, is the largest. It is said that the most powerful Tutsi—the Tutsi elite class—come from Bururi.

Muramvya is another busy market town. It has tea plantations and is a good source of such handicrafts as drums and cowhides. Located northeast of Bujumbura in a mountainous region, Muramvya's Lookout Point offers a breathtaking view.

The tourist industry is in its infancy in Burundi. Foreign visitors are sometimes wary because of the possibility of political strife and violence. But the country has good prospects as a tourist attraction, with scenic mountains and lakes, exotic birds and butterflies, and a pleasant climate in the highlands. Some natural wonders that may attract tourists in the future include Lake Tanganyika, the waterfalls of Nyakayi and Rusumu in the west, and the fabled source of the Nile—the Ruvuvu River in south central Burundi.

Transportation and Communication

Being landlocked in the interior of central Africa has its good points. For example, Burundi suffered less exploitation than some coastal African nations from European powers during the colonial era, and it was protected from slave traders and invaders. But there are drawbacks to being geographically isolated. Transportation and communication are especially difficult, and Burundi does not have the funds to pay for the kinds of services it needs.

Because Burundi is not located on or near the coast, goods cannot be shipped cheaply by sea into and out of the country. The

This shipment of hides will travel across Lake Tanganyika on a steamer and then to the Indian Ocean. Burundi's lack of a seaport makes international trade difficult.

country has no railroads, although plans to build a railroad linking Ugunda, Rwanda, Burundi, and Tanzania are under consideration by the four nations. For the time being, Burundi must depend upon roads and rivers to move goods. Fortunately, Burundi owns part of Lake Tanganyika, where boats travel up and down transporting passengers and goods.

Bujumbura is the starting point and destination for freight. Situated on Lake Tanganyika, it is a hub of activity for the lake's steamers and barges that reach ports in Tanzania and Zaire. Freight can travel overseas from Burundi by two routes: One goes east through Tanzania, and the other goes west through Zaire. Goods traveling the first route are loaded onto boats at Bujumbura and shipped down the lake to Kigoma in Tanzania. There they are loaded onto a train, which goes across Tanzania to the port city of Dar es Salaam on the Indian Ocean. From there, the goods can be transported to international buyers.

The second route goes by boat from Bujumbura across Lake Tanganyika to Kalemi in Zaire. From there, goods are carried by rail to Lobito, a port on the Atlantic Ocean in the country of Angola, or to Beira, an Indian Ocean port in Mozambique. Other routes go north to Rwanda, Uganda, and Kenya. The transportation industry, however, concentrates on the eastern route—the least expensive— for shipping goods.

According to a report prepared by the American embassy in Burundi and published in February 1986, it is becoming more common for Burundians to import and export goods by air freight. In 1983, goods arriving by air freight totaled 4,545 metric tons; departing goods totaled 2,974 metric tons.

Passenger traffic also flies into Bujumbura. The new international airport is capable of handling large jet aircraft. In 1986, 22,032 people flew into Burundi, and 22,374 flew out. Bujumbura Airport is a link between Burundi and other countries of the world. Air Burundi, the national airline, has scheduled flights to Rwanda, Tanzania, and Zaire. It also has flights to Gitega. Burundi has seven other airfields equipped for small aircraft.

A dense network of roads, including highways, dirt roads, and trails, covers the countryside. Of the 3,196 miles (5,144 kilometers) of roads, only 7 percent are paved. About half are dirt roads; others

Age-old methods of transportation are the norm outside the cities of Bujumbura and Gitega.

are topped with gravel or laterite (a reddish rock); asphalt roads are concentrated in the capital. Mountainous terrain makes it hard to build and maintain roads, and during the rainier months, roads are often flooded and washed out.

The number of motor vehicles has been steadily increasing over the years; still, few families own vehicles. Most of the 7,533 cars in Burundi are owned by government workers in the cities. Local travel is done mostly on foot. Bicycles and motorcycles are popular on the road that runs along Lake Tanganyika.

News gets around by word of mouth, as it always has in Burundi. Televisions are quite rare; the country has one set for every 1,207 people. Radios are more numerous—one for every 21 people. The state broadcasting organization controls the airwaves, presenting daily programs in Kirundi, Swahili, French, and English. This organization, called Voix de la Révolution (Voice of the Revolution), was established in 1960.

Although trucks and cars are common in Bujumbura, paved roads are rare outside the cities. Distribution of goods is often time-consuming and dangerous.

In Burundi, as in much of Africa, there is no tradition of written news or history. People passed down knowledge through what is called the oral tradition—telling stories and relaying news and history through speech, songs, and chanting. Drums were used to convey news of a death or to summon people for a gathering. Dance, too, has long been a way of communicating information about the past, about beliefs, and about people's lives.

In terms of modern, western-style communication, Burundi does have a few newspapers and magazines. The press is strictly controlled by the government. Three newspapers are published in Bujumbura: the *Burundi chrétien*, a French weekly published by the Roman Catholic Diocese of Gitega; *Le Renouveau du Burundi*, a French daily paper put out by the Ministry of Information; and *Ubumwe*, a weekly newspaper published in Kirundi. The latter two newspapers have a combined daily circulation of about 20,000. A news agency in Bujumbura puts out a daily news bulletin.

Four magazines are published. The *Bulletin économique et financier*, with economic and financial news, appears every two months. The *Bulletin officiel du Burundi* is monthly; *Le Burundi en images*, a picture magazine, is monthly; and *Culture et sociétés* is published four times a year.

News is closely censored by the government, which does not permit unfavorable news stories or views critical of the president to be published.

With the assistance of the United Nations, the government has attempted to develop Burundi's small but growing fishing industry.

A Desperate Economy

The typical Burundian farmer handles only a very small amount of money each year, lives off the land, and barters—with livestock, produce, and other goods or services—for anything else his or her family needs. The cow, introduced into Burundi by Tutsi cattle herders, has long been "living gold" for the Burundians. Today, both cattle and modern money become involved in traditional exchanges, such as bridewealth.

The cash currency of the country is the Burundi franc, which is worth about four-fifths of a United States penny; 126 FBu (Burundi francs) equal U.S. $1. The Burundi franc is divided into 100 centimes.

Agriculture makes up 63.1 percent of Burundi's total economic production, employs 92 percent of the labor force, and provides 90 percent of exports. The agricultural economy has three forms: subsistence farming, cash crops, and agricultural import substitutions.

Subsistence agriculture is the cultivation of food crops for use within the country. The chief subsistence crops are cassava, sweet potatoes, beans, bananas, corn, and sorghum. Cash crops are grown primarily for export to other countries. Coffee, tea, and cotton are Burundi's three main cash crops, although palms, for oil, and to-

Cattle continue to provide meat, hides, and milk as well as serving as a substitute for money in bartering.

bacco are also grown. Agricultural import substitutions are crops that are introduced so that Burundi no longer has to import them, often at high expense, from other countries. Crops in this category include palm oil, rice, and sugarcane.

Government programs have tried to improve agriculture for several years. Plans have focused on enriching tired soil by using fertilizers, on introducing better varieties of plants, and on preventing erosion. The government has also encouraged growing cash crops, such as coffee, tea, cotton, and tobacco, to bring in foreign currencies and boost the economy.

Bananas account for 50 percent of all subsistence farming. They are used primarily for producing beer. A drought in 1984 had serious consequences for farmers, who experienced a 10.5 percent decline in production that year. Adequate rainfall since then has improved production, but the drought demonstrated how vulnerable Burundi is because of its dependence on agriculture. When the country does not get enough rain, everyone suffers.

Coffee is the single most important source of income for the country, accounting for 85 percent of Burundi's cash-crop earnings on the world market. It has been cultivated since 1930 and is grown almost exclusively by private owners on small plots of land. The dark brew is not a traditional beverage, which means that few Burundians drink it. Burundi exports virtually all its coffee to other countries, primarily in the West. The United States has been a major buyer of Burundian coffee in years past: At one time the U.S. bought half of the supply. In 1984, however, the U.S. bought less than two percent of Burundi's coffee. That year, the European Economic Community (EEC) was the major importer, buying about 70 percent of the coffee. The United States is increasing its imports in the late 1980s, but the EEC continues to import a substantial share.

Tea plantations in both Burundi and Rwanda have been developed with loans from the European Economic Community and other foreign lenders.

Like all agricultural products, coffee is dependent on favorable weather conditions. Also, the price coffee earns is very much affected by the changes in the world market. In a year when many countries have coffee to sell at low prices, Burundi's earnings drop drastically. To decrease dependency on coffee exports, Burundi has been encouraging the development of other export crops — especially tea and cotton.

So far the plan is working well. In 1984, tea production amounted to 15,000 tons, a 46 percent increase over previous years. As yet, tea brings in only a small percentage of foreign money, but Burundian tea, which is of very high quality, fetches high prices on the world market, and the outlook for future production is good. And as tea, unlike coffee, can be harvested almost all year round, tea production will provide more stable jobs for workers.

Like tea production, Burundi's cotton production is on the increase, and the outlook for exports is favorable. In 1984, the country produced more than 6,500 tons of cotton grain; in 1985, that figure increased to more than 7,150 tons. By the 1990s, Burundi hopes to produce 10,000 tons of cotton a year. Currently, the government is hoping for a loan from France to build a cotton-processing factory.

Next in importance after food crops and coffee is animal husbandry, the raising of livestock for hides, milk, and meat. Cattle, sheep, goats, pigs, and poultry are being raised in increasing numbers. Production in this area, however, has been judged unsatisfactory by some economists. While the demand for meat is increasing in the cities and in neighboring countries, most rural Burundians do not seem eager to consume more meat. Meat eating is not an established part of the diet, and it goes against tradition. The Burundians prefer their cattle to be live, countable symbols of wealth. The slaughter of a cow reduces one's visible wealth. Moreover, cows are believed to be close to Imana, the traditional god.

Fish, on the other hand, have long been caught and eaten in certain areas of Burundi. Fish caught in Lake Tanganyika totaled 10,000 tons in 1985. There are three methods of fishing on the lake. The industrial method is carried out in trawlers, or small ships. The native method is carried out in small wooden boats with nets and engines. The traditional method is carried out in man-powered canoes with nets. Unfortunately, fish are too costly for most people to afford (the larger fish especially). Burundi is working on plans with several countries for foreign-aid loans to build fisheries in the interior of Burundi.

Raising poultry is one of many innovations supported by the Burundian government. Such new ventures may help Burundi's burgeoning population avoid starvation.

Minerals are a potentially valuable resource. Burundi has large deposits of nickel (perhaps as much as five percent of the world supply), phosphates, vanadium, and tin. Unfortunately, these minerals are not in great demand at present. The country did export some bastnaesite (a mineral used in making color television sets), but production ended in 1979, when the mining operation became unprofitable. Today, Burundi's principal mining operation involves the cutting of peat, a substance similar to coal that is found in three of Burundi's swamps. It is cut into bricks and, when dried, can be burned as fuel. Experts estimate that Burundi has 200 to 500 million tons of peat in reserve. Although the peat will probably never be exported, it is a good source of fuel, now that wood is extremely scarce.

Passenger ships as well as freighters ply the busy waters of Lake Tanganyika. Most of the fuel for such ships is supplied by Iran.

Burundi has little industry; what there is mostly centers around food processing and the brewing and bottling of beer. Soft drinks, cigarettes, blankets, and footwear are also produced. Burundi's industry has not grown as fast as the government had hoped, despite enormous amounts of money, mostly foreign-aid loans, spent to develop it. Some reasons for the industrial lag are the low demand for manufactured goods, which most Burundians cannot afford; the serious shortage of trained workers; and the reluctance of companies to build plants in Burundi in the face of electrical shortages and the expense of shipping goods.

Burundi imports consumer goods (beverages, clothing, processed foods, textiles), construction materials, and machinery from France, Belgium, Luxembourg, Japan, and West Germany. Burundi's largest supplier of imports is Iran, which supplies most of the country's oil and gasoline. The leading purchasers of Burundian exports are West Germany, Italy, Belgium, Luxembourg, and the United States.

Since independence, Burundi's various governments have announced a series of hopeful plans for economic growth. But the country's overcrowding, poor soil, and constant political turmoil have reduced economic progress to a slow crawl. Despite some good signs, such as the increase in tea production and the development of the peat-cutting industry, Burundi's economy is one of the world's weakest. The country manages to feed itself, but just barely, and malnutrition is not uncommon. Burundians must import twice as much as they export, and they rely on loans and foreign aid. Given the currently poor state of the economy, survival is a struggle. Growth will require miracles in the areas of dedication, honest government, farming and energy technology, and international cooperation.

Elementary school students such as these Tutsi children use their native language, Kirundi, in school. They must learn French to attend high school.

Health, Education, and the Arts

After Burundi became independent in 1962, the United Nations' World Health Organization (WHO) helped set up the new nation's public health services, and some Burundians received medical or nursing training in France and Zaire. Other UN organizations provided funds and training to fight smallpox, tuberculosis, malaria, and malnutrition. Many of these programs continue, but they cannot keep pace with the health needs of a growing but poor population. Malnutrition and the diseases connected with it continue. Measles, diarrhea, malaria, and tuberculosis are the leading causes of death. The average Burundian man can expect to live only 45 years; women have a life expectancy of 48 years. Epidemics of infectious diseases such as cholera are caused by poor sanitation and infected drinking water. Such epidemics occur infrequently, but they kill thousands. Currently, Burundi is working with officials from the World Health Organization to slow the spread of AIDS (acquired immunodeficiency syndrome), which afflicts thousands of men and women in south central Africa.

The government operates some of Burundi's 22 hospitals, 9 maternity clinics, and 100 health facilities. Christian missionaries

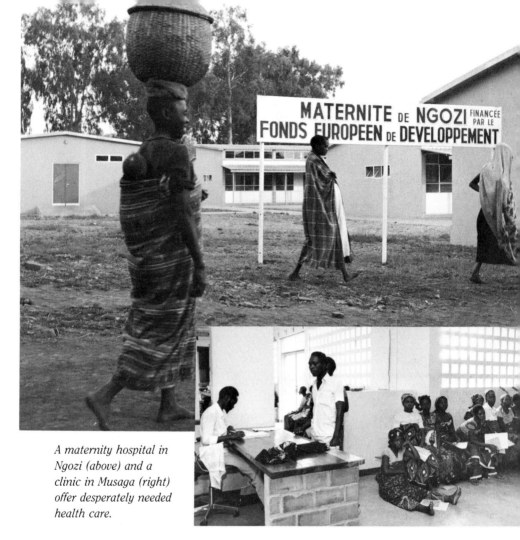

A maternity hospital in Ngozi (above) and a clinic in Musaga (right) offer desperately needed health care.

operate the rest. There is 1 hospital bed for every 792 inhabitants and 1 doctor for every 20,942 inhabitants. In 1986, China sent medical aid to Burundi in the form of drugs and equipment. A team of 12 Chinese medical specialists spent two years in the country, training local health-care workers.

Like its health-care system, Burundi's educational system is struggling against enormous obstacles. The country has only 1,023 primary schools and 62 high schools. There are 47 schools for training in teaching or other job skills and one university. Teachers are in desperately short supply—there are only 9,572 in all the schools in the country. Burundi has a literacy rate of 34 percent—that is, 34 percent of the population over age 10 can read and write.

Before Roman Catholic and Protestant missions set up schools at the turn of the century, boys and girls were taught at home to do certain tasks at certain ages. Formal education began in 1900, when the Roman Catholic Order of the Missionaries of Africa (called the White Fathers) built a mission school. Many more mission schools were established after 1916, when Belgian missionaries entered the scene. These remained the official schools during the Belgian administration. Instruction was given in Kirundi or Swahili until 1948, when French was introduced as the official language of instruction.

Today, Burundian children in primary schools learn in Kirundi and study French; classes in secondary schools are taught in French. Educational aid reaches Burundi through United Nations agencies, the Peace Corps, and other sources.

In 1960, a university was established in Bujumbura. Today, the University of Burundi has about 1,800 students and 300 faculty members. The academic year runs from October to June. Various schools within the university teach letters and humanities, economic and administrative sciences, natural sciences, law, medicine, psychology and education, agriculture, and physical education.

Several technical colleges teach skills such as drafting. This draftsman prepares plans for a refugee camp.

In addition, there are two technical colleges in Bujumbura. The Lycée Technique, founded in 1949, trains apprentices, craftsmen, and professional workers in mechanics, masonry (bricklaying), carpentry, and electrical assembly; 450 students were training there in 1980. The Centre Social et Éducatif, established in 1957, trains students in crafts, photography, and mechanics. It had 75 students in 1980.

The importance of teaching has long been recognized by those who first brought formal education to Burundi—the Roman Catholic missionaries. The White Fathers were told by papal authorities in Rome, "Build churches and schools, but if you must make a choice between the two, build the schools." Today, the state provides free education to all Burundian children, but only 25 percent of primary-school-age children attend, and only 4 percent of the eligible children attend secondary school.

One reason that many children fail to attend school is that there are too few schools, but the biggest reason is that many rural families do not believe that their children need formal education. It is most common for families to follow tradition, keeping the children at home to work in the fields, tend the cattle, or take care of their younger brothers and sisters.

The Lively Arts

Dance, music, storytelling, and craftwork are a way of life, a part of the Burundians' daily experience. The most intricate and beautiful baskets are not housed in museums; music is not limited to the concert hall. It is true that there is an important museum of traditional arts in Gitega, the ancient capital. And Tutsi dancers have performed on stages around the world. But the majority of Burundi's artists are the people themselves; their homes are both stage and gallery. Artistic expression enlivens each family or social gathering and plays an essential role in every ritual from birth to death.

A tribal dancer faces an audience of other performers clad in traditional robes and paints.

On very basic levels, artistic expression is highly valued. Learning to use the Kirundi language in a poetic fashion has long been a tradition. Until the turn of the century, when European influence became established, there was no written way to record stories and history. Literature was handed down in many spoken forms: poetry, fables, legends, proverbs, riddles, and ballads. People especially eloquent in this "oral literature" were—and are—held in high regard. They are models for younger people, who learn the tales in turn and pass them along. Many of the old stories are epic poems about cattle. Storytellers also share stories about events that happened to their relatives or to themselves. Different storytellers may present different versions of the same event, which makes the event more interesting, more personal, and more enjoyable because of the perspectives offered.

The words in speech, poems, and songs are considered especially moving and powerful if they contain the skillful use of indirect descriptions and figures of speech. The more subtle and delicate the allusion, the more beautiful the language. For example, a storyteller who wanted to indicate that it was a hot summer night might mention the drone of summer insects and the stillness of the air, rather than saying, "It was a hot summer night."

Poems often turn into songs. When people gather for any reason—whether with family members alone or while entertaining guests—someone is bound to begin playing an instrument. With music playing in the background, the storyteller's rhythmic words become the lyrics of a song. Burundi tradition has a song for every mood and every occasion, as well as a variety of ways in which songs are sung.

Imvyino is a group song with a short refrain and a strong beat. Everyone can join the refrain. Families that sing imvyino at a gathering often dance too, and sometimes one person begins to make up new verses. This is especially entertaining to the listeners because the lyrics are colorful and often related to the main event of the day. It is also a way of transmitting news to the entire clan.

Another type of song is *indirimbo*, which expresses quiet feelings on a number of themes. Indirimbo is not a group song like imvyino but rather is sung by a soloist or a handful of people. *Bilito* is typically a sentimental, melancholy song associated with women. *Kwishongora* is a men's song. It has rhythmic shouts and high-pitched trills best sung by very clear voices.

Of all the music produced by Burundian voices, "whispered singing" is perhaps the best known. Whispered singing is a technique of singing along with instruments, but quietly enough to allow the subtle sounds of traditional instruments to be clearly heard. Men perform whispered singing to the *inanga* and the *idono*, two instruments that are also used in a variety of ways other than to accompany singing.

The inanga is a zitherlike instrument; it is unlike a guitar or lute because it has no neck. Six to eight strings are stretched across a flat piece of wood or bark that is hollowed out to resemble a long oval bowl. The musician may squat on the ground next to the inanga, plucking the strings, which are held in place by notches at either end. Men of all classes play the inanga, for their own pleasure or for that of their listeners. Unlike the drums of ancient Burundi, the inanga was not traditionally reserved for men of the Tutsi elite. In 1970, the inanga was featured on a recording entitled *Musique du Burundi* (Music of Burundi). The album won first prize in an international contest in Paris. It was the first recording of Burundian music to be commercially available.

The idono is another stringed instrument. Shaped like a hunting bow, the idono has a single string stretched tightly across the bow by a ring connected to a wooden "bowl." A musician plays different notes by moving the ring up and down the bowl, while holding the instrument in front of the body with the chamber next to the chest.

Fifes and flutes are also popular instruments, particularly fifes. Both are made of wooden tubes; fifes are shorter in length. One flute, the *ikihusehama*, resembles a clarinet. Usually these wind instruments are played in orchestral groups together with drums.

Drums have long held a special place in the hearts of the Burundians, both as rhythm instruments and as symbols of power and prestige. The mwami's drum was the ultimate symbol of power and was considered sacred in ancient Burundi. Young men selected to play this drum were the envy of all others. One drum is played by several men at one time, and then each man takes a turn at playing solo. Usually the group plays until each drummer has had a chance to express himself with his own rhythms. On the award-winning recording *Musique du Burundi*, an ensemble of 25 men plays a drum, first together and then all 25 of them in turn. Drums are heard at every traditional holiday celebration. The drummers create the rhythms to which dancers perform, and sometimes they themselves become the dancers.

Dance cannot easily be separated from music in Burundi, nor can it be considered apart from daily life. Dance exists on many levels, from everyday dance to the ritualistic movements performed only at special events. Dance is essential to all family and ceremonial gatherings.

Although many types of dance are native to Burundi, not many are known outside the country. An exception is the Tutsi dances, which are performed by a highly trained elite corps of professional dancers—all are male and quite tall. Their height and appearance are striking: They wear leopard fur around their waists and head-dresses made from the light-colored fur of the colobus monkey. The Tutsi dancers perform in graceful unison, a spirited display accented by intricate, formal movements and majestic leaps into the air. The effect is exciting, full of drama, and stirring to those fortunate enough to view it. Nowadays, tourists can arrange to see Tutsi dancers perform, but for more than 400 years, during the long reign of the Tutsi kings, the dancers performed primarily for the royal court.

Female dancers perform a fertility dance as part of the 1962 independence celebration.

Handicrafts

As with music and dance, handicrafts such as baskets, ironwork, and leather goods have always been part of daily life. They are meant to be used, although the most prized items may be reserved for special occasions. When guests come to visit, for example, the family's best basket may be used to hold a beer pot for the guests. In former days, most handicrafts were simply not for sale, although sometimes a particular item might have been traded for a cow. The household with a large number of skillfully made baskets was judged to be higher on the social scale than one with few baskets or poorly made ones. Today, many handcrafted items are displayed in markets to be sold for money.

Historically, Tutsi women made many of the most beautiful baskets, with the help of servants. In general, women make Burundi's baskets, and talented basket makers are paid well to teach their techniques to young women. The raw materials for this craft are the fibers of the papyrus root, bast (a strong woody fiber), and banana leaves. These are woven into baskets or coiled into different shapes. Some are watertight cups, lids for the gourd bottles that hold beer, and bowls. Some are placed atop the head to hold bundles for carrying, and others store foods and seasonings, such as salt and pepper.

Burundian baskets tend to be yellow or tan in color, with geometric designs woven in by means of strips dyed mauve or black. Mud from the marshes provides the dyes. Some typical patterns are zigzags, triangles, and narrow strips in a pattern like the natural pattern of banana leaves. Patterning a basket after the banana leaf symbolizes the importance of banana beer in social relations. Some ornamental baskets use white and blue beads as well.

The geometric patterns seen in baskets appear in other handcrafted objects, such as leather goods and iron items. One special item is the lance, or spear. Made of iron by blacksmiths, lances originally were used in hunting and in war, carried as status symbols,

Burundian handicrafts may be enjoyed as works of art, but they were first created to be used. Drums were part of religious ceremonies and provided the music for social gatherings; baskets held food and beer; and everyday tools such as hoes were enlivened with carvings and paint.

and held as part of traditional dress on special occasions. When the head of a family died, his lance was handed to his oldest son to show the transfer of power to a new head of the family. The lance was lethal, designed to plunge into flesh, rendering prey incapable of twisting away.

Other handcrafted iron goods seen in Burundi are decorations for pots and baskets. Pottery itself is not as well developed as other handicrafts. Wooden bowls and vessels of basketry are more common than clay pots. The Twa, however, make some ceramics.

Western influence through the art shops in Catholic mission schools has had an effect on the decorative arts. At one time, the traditional geometric designs began to be replaced by the realistic figures of Western-style art. Traditionalists urged Burundian artists to return to their classic geometric designs.

The visitor to Burundi will find handcrafted works for sale in market towns and in the open-air markets of Bujumbura and Gitega. The National Museum of Gitega, founded in 1955, contains folk art, historical artifacts, and a library. There is a "living museum" in Bujumbura that sponsors exhibits about the people's daily life. It was founded in 1977 as part of the Center of Burundi Civilization, which is affiliated with the Ministry of Youth, Sport, and Culture. The center also has an open-air theater, a botanical garden, a music pavilion, and a crafts village.

A 16-month-old Hutu baby from Burundi is carried to a hospital in neighboring Rwanda. He was wounded with a bayonet in fighting between Burundi's Hutu and Tutsi in August of 1988.

The Question of Survival

One of the 20 poorest nations in the world, Burundi is troubled by a burgeoning population and inadequate food supplies. It also has serious problems associated with the long-lasting hatred between the Hutu and the Tutsi peoples and with the instability of its government.

Agriculture is the main economic activity. Coffee will undoubtedly continue to bring in the most foreign revenue. Tea is also a very promising crop. After coffee and tea, cotton and animal hides are the leading exports. Yet all of these exports combined cannot begin to pay for the petroleum, machinery, and consumer goods the country imports. And subsistence agriculture is stretched to the limit now; as the population increases and the productivity of the eroded soil decreases, hunger will worsen. Famine and starvation have haunted other African nations in recent years—Burundi could suffer the same fate.

Burundi's cool uplands are pleasant, and some of its scenery is spectacular. Tourism could become an important part of the economy, but there are obstacles. Deforestation and the loss of wildlife have made the country less attractive. It is hard to get around, with few transportation choices and mostly dirt roads of poor quality that become muddy and impassable during certain seasons. Coups, civil wars, and other forms of political strife also discourage tourists. Both tourism and trade would benefit from a railroad to link Burundi with Tanzania and the Indian Ocean. The shortage of funds has prevented such a railroad from being built. For transportation, Burundi must be careful to maintain good relations with neighboring countries — Zaire, Tanzania, Rwanda, and Uganda. Civil war or disturbance in any of those countries, or a war between Burundi and any of them, could give the death blow to Burundi's ailing economy.

On July 1, 1962, the Belgian flag was lowered for the last time in Bujumbura.

Burundi may be torn by renewed internal strife in the years to come, according to some specialists in African history and politics. The imbalance of power between the powerful Tutsi minority and the powerless Hutu majority could bring about uprisings and massacres similar to those of the early 1970s. Most positions of authority in government and the military are held by Tutsi. Hutu representation remains very low. Now that the constitution and voting rights have been suspended by a military dictatorship, the dissatisfaction of the Hutu—and the potential for renewed violence—are likely to increase.

Ahead lie many challenges for this small republic. The government is trying to overcome some of these challenges before they begin by borrowing money from abroad and by seeking foreign aid to boost the economy and improve agriculture. Other challenges are met as they crop up. For example, the epidemic of AIDS in south central Africa has hit Burundi hard, although the government will not release figures on the number of cases. The World Health Organization has researchers and medical staff in Burundi to establish programs aimed at preventing and treating the disease. Other troublesome diseases exist in Burundi, many of which have been eliminated in more developed nations. Preventive health care, especially programs focusing on nutrition, will have important long-term effects on the health and life expectancy of Burundi's people—if the government and the international aid agencies have the funds to carry them out properly.

Education also cries out for improvement. With its low literacy rate of 34 percent, Burundi cannot expect to develop rapidly. People must be trained as teachers, civil servants, economists, factory workers, computer operators, and so forth. Perhaps women will receive better educational opportunities in the future. At present, most girls stay home to perform domestic chores, many of which are vital to keeping the family alive—preparing food and carrying water, for

Burundians raise the red, white, and green flag of independent Burundi, a symbol of pride and hope.

example. The same is true of boys, who must stay home to work in the fields or tend livestock and poultry. Theirs is a terrible dilemma—they live in a country where education is free, but the "cost" of attending school may jeopardize their family's existence.

In the area of land reform, the Bagaza government tried to bring about change by forcing some Tutsi lords to give over much of their land to Hutu peasants. Hutu refugees who return to Burundi are given land on which to settle. But although the feudal ubugabire relationship has been abolished, much of the land is still owned by the Tutsi, and many Hutu continue to work for their former masters because they have nothing else to do. Change is slow, and it is unclear whether Buyoya's government will support further changes in land ownership.

The Burundian people live much as they have for centuries, although Hutu and Tutsi relations have changed outwardly. People till the soil, tend livestock, observe traditional and religious holidays (and now Independence Day and other state holidays as well), and count on hard work to get by season after season, year after year. Whether their lives will be easier in the future, whether many of them will even survive their country's present problems, depends upon many things: the stability of Buyoya's government, the preservation of the uneasy truce between Tutsi and Hutu, the control of AIDS, the continued support of foreign aid—and good rainfall for the crops.

◄ G L O S S A R Y ►

Bahinza A Hutu word for "those who cause things to grow." The bahinza were the rulers of the Hutu kingdoms before the arrival of the Tutsi.

Bast A strong woody fiber used by Tutsi women for basket weaving.

Bastnaesite A mineral used in making color television sets.

Bilito A sentimental or sad song, usually sung by a woman.

Cassava Also called manioc; a starchy plant whose roots can be ground into flour. It is a staple food in much of Africa.

Congo-Nile Crest A series of mountain ridges in western Burundi that form the watershed between the Congo and Nile river systems. Streams from the eastern side of the ridge flow into the Nile; streams from the western side flow into the Congo.

Ganwa Princes related to the *bami* (kings) in the Tutsi monarchy. The ganwa were extremely powerful within their own domains and sometimes competed with or fought against the bami.

Idono A musical instrument shaped like a hunting bow with a wooden sounding bowl attached. The player cradles the bowl against his chest and moves the string across it.

Ikihusehama A flute that resembles a clarinet.

Imana The supreme being of traditional Burundian belief.

Imvyino	A group song with short verses and a strong beat.
Inanga	A stringed instrument like a harp or zither.
Indirimbo	A song for a soloist or small group of singers, usually restrained in tone.
Inka	Kirundi for "cattle."
Karyenda	The sacred drum of the mwami.
Kubandwa	A festival to celebrate the grain harvest. It includes ceremonial chanting and dancing.
Kuvamukiriri	A child's naming ceremony. The paternal grandfather gives the child a proper name, a family name, and one or two nicknames. Christian families baptize their children at the ceremony.
Kwashiorkor	A disease that results from a lack of protein. It can be fatal, and survivors suffer liver damage and other diseases. Kwashiorkor is one of Africa's greatest health problems.
Mwami	The title of the Tutsi kings of Burundi.
Ubugabire	The contract, usually based on wealth in the form of cattle, that bound a Hutu peasant to his Tutsi overlord in a feudal social system.
Umuganuro	A fertility ceremony in which sorghum seeds are planted in the hope of a good harvest. Umuganuro was traditionally a time when the Tutsi ganwa and the Hutu peasants sealed their contracts of ubugabire.
Ujusohor	A ceremony in which a six-day-old baby is presented to his or her clan, and the mother receives gifts and flowers.
UPRONA	National Progress and Unity party, the ruling and only legal political party in Burundi.
Watusi	Another term for Tutsi.

◄INDEX►

PICTURE CREDITS